DATE DUE

DEMCO 128-8155

MORGAN FREEMAN

MORGAN FREEMAN

❧

Gina De Angelis

CHELSEA HOUSE PUBLISHERS
Philadelphia

Chelsea House Publishers

Editor in Chief	Stephen Reginald
Production Manager	Pamela Loos
Director of Photography	Judy L. Hasday
Art Director	Sara Davis
Managing Editor	James D. Gallagher
Senior Production Editor	LeeAnne Gelletly

Staff for MORGAN FREEMAN

Senior Editor	Therese De Angelis
Associate Art Director	Takeshi Takahashi
Designer	21st Century Publishing and Communications
Picture Researcher	Sandy Jones
Cover Illustrator	Cliff Spohn
Cover Designer	Keith Trego

The Chelsea House World Wide Website address is
http://www.chelseahouse.com

First Printing

1 3 5 7 9 8 6 4 2

Library of Congress Cataloging-in-Pubication Data

De Angelis, Gina.
  Morgan Freeman / Gina De Angelis.
    pp.   cm. — (Black Americans of achievement)
  Filmography: p.
Includes bibliographical references and index.
Summary: Traces the childhood and acting career of the Oscar-nominated star of such films as "Driving Miss Daisy" and "Seven."
ISBN 0-7910-4963-9 (hc) 0-7910-4964-7 (pbk.)
1. Freeman, Morgan—Juvenile literature. 2. Actors—United States—Biography—Juvenile literature. 3. Afro-American actors—United States—Biography—Juvenile literature. [1. Freeman, Morgan. 2. Actors and actresses. 3. Afro-Americans—Biography.] I. Title. II. Series.
PN2287.F683D43 1999
791.43'028'092—dc21
[B]   99-18478
                                                                       CIP
                                                                        AC

Frontis: Years of hard work and perseverance have made Morgan Freeman one of the most popular actors in Hollywood today.

CONTENTS

BLACK AMERICANS OF ACHIEVEMENT

HENRY AARON
baseball great

KAREEM ABDUL-JABBAR
basketball great

MUHAMMAD ALI
heavyweight champion

RICHARD ALLEN
*religious leader and
social activist*

MAYA ANGELOU
author

LOUIS ARMSTRONG
musician

ARTHUR ASHE
tennis great

JOSEPHINE BAKER
entertainer

JAMES BALDWIN
author

TYRA BANKS
model

BENJAMIN BANNEKER
scientist and mathematician

AMIRI BARAKA
poet and playwright

COUNT BASIE
bandleader and composer

ROMARE BEARDEN
artist

JAMES BECKWOURTH
frontiersman

MARY MCLEOD BETHUNE
educator

GEORGE WASHINGTON
CARVER
botanist

CHARLES CHESNUTT
author

JOHNNIE COCHRAN
lawyer

BILL COSBY
entertainer

PAUL CUFFE
merchant and abolitionist

MILES DAVIS
musician

FATHER DIVINE
religious leader

FREDERICK DOUGLASS
abolitionist editor

CHARLES DREW
physician

W. E. B. DU BOIS
scholar and activist

PAUL LAURENCE DUNBAR
poet

DUKE ELLINGTON
bandleader and composer

RALPH ELLISON
author

JULIUS ERVING
basketball great

LOUIS FARRAKHAN
political activist

ELLA FITZGERALD
singer

MORGAN FREEMAN
actor

MARCUS GARVEY
black nationalist leader

JOSH GIBSON
baseball great

WHOOPI GOLDBERG
entertainer

CUBA GOODING JR.
actor

ALEX HALEY
author

PRINCE HALL
social reformer

JIMI HENDRIX
musician

MATTHEW HENSON
explorer

GREGORY HINES
performer

BILLIE HOLIDAY
singer

LENA HORNE
entertainer

WHITNEY HOUSTON
singer and actress

LANGSTON HUGHES
poet

ZORA NEALE HURSTON
author

JANET JACKSON
singer

JESSE JACKSON *civil-rights leader and politician*	SPIKE LEE *filmmaker*	CHARLIE PARKER *musician*	TINA TURNER *entertainer*
MICHAEL JACKSON *entertainer*	CARL LEWIS *champion athlete*	ROSA PARKS *civil-rights leader*	DENMARK VESEY *slave revolt leader*
SAMUEL L. JACKSON *actor*	JOE LOUIS *heavyweight champion*	COLIN POWELL *military leader*	ALICE WALKER *author*
T. D. JAKES *religious leader*	RONALD MCNAIR *astronaut*	PAUL ROBESON *singer and actor*	MADAM C. J. WALKER *entrepreneur*
JACK JOHNSON *heavyweight champion*	MALCOLM X *militant black leader*	JACKIE ROBINSON *baseball great*	BOOKER T. WASHINGTON *educator*
MAGIC JOHNSON *basketball great*	BOB MARLEY *musician*	CHRIS ROCK *comedian/actor*	DENZEL WASHINGTON *actor*
SCOTT JOPLIN *composer*	THURGOOD MARSHALL *Supreme Court justice*	DIANA ROSS *entertainer*	J. C. WATTS *politician*
BARBARA JORDAN *politician*	TONI MORRISON *author*	WILL SMITH *actor*	VANESSA WILLIAMS *singer and actress*
MICHAEL JORDAN *basketball great*	ELIJAH MUHAMMAD *religious leader*	CLARENCE THOMAS *Supreme Court justice*	OPRAH WINFREY *entertainer*
CORETTA SCOTT KING *civil-rights leader*	EDDIE MURPHY *entertainer*	SOJOURNER TRUTH *antislavery activist*	TIGER WOODS *golf star*
MARTIN LUTHER KING JR. *civil-rights leader*	JESSE OWENS *champion athlete*	HARRIET TUBMAN *antislavery activist*	RICHARD WRIGHT *author*
LEWIS LATIMER *scientist*	SATCHEL PAIGE *baseball great*	NAT TURNER *slave revolt leader*	

ON
ACHIEVEMENT

———— ❧ ————

Coretta Scott King

Before you begin this book, I hope you will ask yourself what the word *excellence* means to you. I think it's a question we should all ask, and keep asking as we grow older and change. Because the truest answer to it should never change. When you think of excellence, perhaps you think of success at work; or of becoming wealthy; or meeting the right person, getting married, and having a good family life.

Those goals are worth striving for, but there is a better way to look at excellence. As Martin Luther King Jr. said in one of his last sermons, "I want you to be first in love. I want you to be first in moral excellence. I want you to be first in generosity. If you want to be important, wonderful. If you want to be great, wonderful. But recognize that he who is greatest among you shall be your servant."

My husband knew that the true meaning of achievement is service. When I met him, in 1952, he was already ordained as a Baptist minister and was working toward a doctoral degree at Boston University. I was studying at the New England Conservatory and dreamed of accomplishments in music. We married a year later, and after I graduated the following year we moved to Montgomery, Alabama. We didn't know it then, but our notions of achievement were about to undergo a dramatic change.

You may have read or heard about what happened next. What began with the boycott of a local bus line grew into a national crusade, and by the time he was assassinated in 1968 my husband had fashioned a black movement powerful enough to shatter forever the practice of racial segregation. What you may not have read about is where he learned to resist injustice without compromising his religious beliefs.

He adopted a strategy of nonviolence from a man of a different race, who lived in a different country and even practiced a different religion. The man was Mahatma Gandhi, the great leader of India, who devoted his life to serving humanity in the spirit of love and nonviolence. It was in these principles that Martin discovered his method for social reform. More than anything else, those two principles were the key to his achievements.

These books are about African Americans who served society through the excellence of their achievements. They form part of the rich history of black men and women in America—a history of stunning accomplishments in every field of human endeavor, from literature and art to science, industry, education, diplomacy, athletics, jurisprudence, even polar exploration.

Not all of the people in this history had the same ideals, but I think you will find that all of them had something in common. Like Martin Luther King Jr., they all decided to become "drum majors" and serve humanity. In that principle—whether it was expressed in books, inventions, or song—they found a goal and a guide outside themselves that showed them a way to serve others instead of living only for themselves.

Reading the stories of these courageous men and women not only helps us discover the principles that we will use to guide our own lives; it also teaches us about our black heritage and about America itself. It is crucial for us to know the heroes and heroines of our history and to realize that the price we paid in our struggle for equality in America was dear. But we must also understand that we have gotten as far as we have partly because America's democratic system and ideals made it possible.

We are still struggling with racism and prejudice. But the great men and women in this series are a tribute to the spirit of the country in which they have flourished. And that makes their stories special and worth knowing.

1

"I WANTED TO *FLY*"

T HE MISSISSIPPI SUN didn't burn through the woods, but hiking made the boys feel dusty and hot. The pond looked cool and inviting, and the boys, keyed up from their field trip, jumped in and began racing one another to the far shore. One of the teens reached the shore and looked back for his friend, a thin boy who was well-known in town and at school. He was a member of the glee club, the debating team, the school band, and especially the drama club. But the thin boy wasn't there anymore. The boy on shore was certain his friend had jumped in after him—he saw him swimming. But then the thin boy must have fallen behind.

In reality, the thin boy had sunk. "When I got halfway I couldn't go any farther," the boy remembered years later. "I remember thinking, I'll just go down to the bottom for a minute and rest. I went down and down, but there didn't seem to be any bottom, and the next thing I know I was at the surface and three people were pulling me out."

Morgan Freeman's life had been saved.

"The day after," Freeman continued in a 1978 interview with *New Yorker* magazine, "I couldn't move, and they discovered I had malnutrition. I developed pneumonia and an abscessed lung. I was in the hospital two weeks, and my mother nursed me back [to health], and, as she always did in bad times, [she] only collapsed when it was over."

Critics showered praise on Morgan Freeman for his role as the president of the United States in the 1998 film Deep Impact. *The award-winning actor "should run for president after playing the perfect one here," one reviewer gushed.*

11

Morgan Freeman's life easily could have ended in a Mississippi pond when he was a boy, if not for the intervention of friends who saved him from drowning.

Morgan Freeman was the fourth child of Mayme Edna Revere Freeman and Morgan Porterfield Freeman, born on June 1, 1937, in Memphis, Tennessee. His family didn't stay long in Memphis, however. Their roots were in northwestern Mississippi in the area known as the Delta, a region with very rich soil but a great division between a few very rich residents and many poor people.

When Morgan was two years old, he and his younger sister, Iris Virginia, were sent to Charleston, Mississippi, to live with their paternal grandmother, Evelyn Freeman. Mayme and Morgan Porterfield Freeman, like many black Americans in the Deep South during the first half of the 20th century, moved north with Morgan's two older brothers to Chicago, Illinois. There they lived with Mayme's cousins and their children. Mayme held jobs teaching and working as a nurse's aide; Morgan Sr. was a barber and odd-jobber.

Morgan Freeman and his family were part of the greatest internal migration in United States history. "Jim Crow" laws passed in the early 1890s in the Deep South made racial segregation legal. From that time until 1920, the number of murders of blacks by white lynch mobs increased exponentially as white southerners sought, in their own ugly words, to "keep the niggers down." World War I, which began in 1914, helped to spur factory production, but slowed the immigration of Europeans into the United States. As a result, northern employers found their immigrant work force depleted and were suddenly more willing to hire black workers. For millions of blacks during this period, conditions in the North, though far from ideal, were a great improvement over the hardships and legal discrimination they experienced in the South.

The first blacks to migrate to the North spread the news about employment and educational opportunities to friends and relatives still living in the South. Black railroad employees who worked on north-to-south routes and northern-based black newspapers like the Chicago *Defender* also helped get the word out. These sources praised the liberating and exhilarating way of life to be had in the North. City life seemed bright and appealing, especially to the

This 1938 photograph shows a Mississippi shanty owned by an African-American family. The shack had once been slave quarters on a plantation. Because of discrimination and other hardships in the South, millions of blacks moved to northern cities such as Chicago during the first half of the 20th century. Among them were Morgan Freeman and his sister, Iris, who joined their parents and older brothers there in 1943.

youngest generation of southerners, many of whom had no desire to stay in the South and work land that they did not own.

Faced with a dwindling labor force, white southern employers tried hard to keep blacks from leaving. Many of them enlisted the help of local police and white citizens. Migrants were sometimes arrested at train stations and charged with "vagrancy"—a violation that was used to prevent blacks from traveling out of the region. Despite arrests and other obstacles, however, blacks continued to migrate to the North. Black families and friends in the North provided a network of information, encouragement, and concrete assistance like housing. It is estimated that half a million black southerners journeyed to northern cities, including Chicago, between 1910 and 1920.

Chicago was a particularly popular destination for southern blacks from Mississippi, Alabama, Arkansas, Tennessee, and Louisiana because of its location on the rail lines from these areas. But millions of southern blacks traveled to other northern cities as well, including Detroit, Cleveland, Cincinnati, New York, Philadelphia, Pittsburgh, Newark, and Baltimore.

Many migrants found that although the North had no racial segregation laws, prejudice was still strong. As in other northern cities, Chicago's working-class neighborhoods were populated largely by Irish, Italian, Polish, and other European immigrants, and bordered the predominantly black neighborhoods. In Chicago, blacks settled in the area known as the South Side, and because of the fierce competition for jobs among immigrants and newly arrived southerners, blacks learned not to cross the invisible lines between their area and nearby neighborhoods.

Friction between "old settlers"—blacks who had been born and raised in Chicago and considered themselves northern—and the new, southern, "countrified" blacks was also evident. The North was culturally different from the South, which had been established on an agricultural economy. Most of the "exodusters," as black migrants from the South were called, had to adjust to the strange rhythm of factory machines rather than the weather and seasons of farm work they had been accustomed to. They also learned to adjust to the noise, bustle, and impersonal nature of urban life.

Despite the difficulties, most migrants from the South chose to stay in the North. As a result, vibrant black communities developed in these northern cities. By 1930, Chicago's South Side was occupied almost exclusively by blacks. Not only did people tend to settle in familiar groups, but also building owners in other areas often refused to rent or sell to blacks.

Another great exodus of black southerners took place after the Great Depression and during World War II. It is estimated that more than 5.5 million black Americans moved north between 1930 and 1970. Large influxes of new residents to northern cities had enormous effects on housing, education, industry, culture, politics, and every other facet of city life.

Although Chicago was known to many black southerners during the Great Migration as "the Promised Land," Morgan Freeman says that his family was among those who "found the promised land not so promising." When Morgan was six years old, his grandmother Evelyn Freeman died, and he and Iris Virginia left Mississippi to live with their parents in Chicago. The move marked the beginning of an unsettling time for Morgan. He still recalls the train trip north and his arrival in Chicago with his sister: "We arrived in the dead of winter, and I couldn't believe how unfriendly the weather was—the bitterness of it, the unyielding quality of the cold, as if it was after *you*."

After about six months, Mayme, Morgan, and Iris Virginia moved to Greenwood, Mississippi, to live with Mayme's mother, Lenora Greenlee Revere. "My father stayed in Chicago," says Morgan, "which was just as well, because he and my mother just didn't get along, no matter how often they tried. I never did see that much of him—I thought of my stepfather as my father." Morgan Porterfield Freeman gradually disappeared from his son's life; he would die in 1961 of alcohol-related causes.

In Mississippi, the Freeman children attended a small one-room school while their mother worked in a nearby town as a teacher. They were there less than three years when Mayme decided to return to Chicago with Morgan and Iris. At first, they lived in

a single room with a gas stove, and Mayme worked night shifts as a nurse's aide. But they never stayed in one place for long. Morgan Freeman generally avoids talking about this period of his life, but he does recall how difficult it was and how rootless he felt: "All we did in Chicago was move," he remembers. "The window sills were our freezer, and once we lived in a building that stood by itself in an empty lot."

Some of Morgan's best memories of this time are of the teachers who encouraged him and pushed him to study harder. He remembers one in particular who

A photo of the frozen Chicago River in winter shows a river barge locked in the ice. When six-year-old Morgan arrived in Chicago, he "couldn't believe how unfriendly the weather was—the bitterness of it, the unyielding quality of the cold." Adjusting to city life equally difficult: "All we did in Chicago was move," he recalled years later.

had "a voice like [husky-voiced film actress] Lauren Bacall." He never forgot the assurances of teachers like her: "When a teacher tells you that you're going to make it, that you've got what it takes, all you can do is keep going. . . . When your teachers are constantly telling you that you're really something, then you feel like something," he told an interviewer for the *Washington Post* in 1989.

Some aspects of living in a tough neighborhood seemed unavoidable—such as becoming affiliated with a street gang. "My gang was called the Spiders," Freeman said in 1978. "I was never really a full-fledged member, but I was doing a lot of stealing and conning all the same." He did his best to avoid gang fights because he was never drawn to violence. But he couldn't avoid joining the Spiders. "You live in a neighborhood like that, you can't survive without belonging," he says. Because school was the one place where he knew he could "shine," he never missed a class. "I was personally happy with books," he told the *Washington Post* in 1989. "I didn't *want* to fight." By concentrating on his schoolwork, Morgan, a sensitive kid who didn't like gang fights because he didn't like to cause pain, somehow managed to survive a succession of tough Chicago neighborhoods.

In 1948, Mayme moved with Morgan and Iris Virginia to Gary, Indiana. Soon after, however, she became seriously ill, and her mother came to take them back to Greenwood, Mississippi. Although many of the early migrant children from the South were placed in lower school grades when they enrolled in northern schools, the opposite happened to Morgan. Despite his excellent grades in Chicago, he was put back a year in Mississippi. "They gave me a test in Greenwood that had a lot of Mississippi history and things I hadn't studied in Chicago. . . . I was crushed," he says. "But then I started acting."

Morgan's first acting experience had been the title role in the third-grade performance of *Little Boy*

Blue in Chicago, but he didn't really "take" to acting until a few years later. Meanwhile, however, the studious boy developed an interest in the movies. "The first movie I remember seeing was *King Kong*," he told *US* magazine in 1997, "and it really affected me. I had nightmares for a long time. I remember I was [hiding] down under the seats with all that sticky taffy stuff."

Before long, Morgan Freeman was hooked. He went to the theater nearly every day, earning the cost of admission by selling milk, soda, and beer bottles for a few cents each. World War II had ended

A scene from the 1933 movie King Kong, the first feature film that Morgan Freeman recalls seeing. He later said that although the film frightened him—"I had nightmares for a long time," he admitted—he became an enthusiastic movie-goer from that time on.

only a few years earlier, and many films focused on war and glamorized the American armed forces. Morgan daydreamed in school about flying P-51 Mustangs or F-86 Sabre jets. His movie heroes, he says, were Gary Cooper, Spencer Tracy, and Sidney Poitier, the only successful black actor of the time, who "pick[ed] all the roles that I wanted."

Morgan Freeman was one of many fans who admired the smooth and talented Poitier, who is credited with being the first black leading man in Hollywood. He opened the door for other black actors and actresses to a white-dominated film industry that had admitted few blacks.

In retrospect, Morgan declares, "I was born to be an actor. I've always been a showoff." But the beginning of his acting career was hardly the result of careful planning or even destiny. In 1950, when Morgan was in seventh grade, he had a classmate named Barbara, "the class princess, as nice as you please." He wanted to get her attention, so he pulled her chair out from under her. "Sure enough, I got attention," he said:

> The teacher grabbed me by the nape of the neck, lifted me onto my toes, and marched me down the hall. I thought for sure I was gonna be 'xpelled. But he opens this door and flings me into this room, and there's this English teacher and he asks me, "You ever done any actin'?" Well, under the circumstances, I'm quick to say yes.

> Well, we do this play [for a state drama competition] 'bout a family with a wounded son just home from the war—I play his kid brother. We win the district championship, we win the state championship, and dadgummit, I'm chosen as best actor. All 'cause I pull this chair out from under Barbara.

Today, after earning dozens of prestigious acting nominations and awards, Morgan says he still has that medal.

Freeman credits another teacher, Leola Gregory Williams at Threadgill High School in Greenwood, with placing him on the path to the theater early on. Miss Williams caught him flirting with girls and declared, "Morgan, you about a mess!" She encouraged him to take up theater as an outlet for his rowdy adolescent behavior. Morgan's school won the state title for drama again in 1952 and 1954.

What did Morgan's mother think of him becoming an actor? Mayme Freeman was "all for it," Morgan says. "She was always telling me when I was a kid, 'Boy, I'm going to take you to Hollywood'—I must have heard that I don't know how many times. And she was always my best audience in school, sitting up front laughing and crying."

"Then," he says wryly of his near-drowning and his stay in the hospital, "if I didn't top that by up and nearly dying." The active and energetic youngster had often neglected to eat, "because I never had any money and I was never much of an eater anyway." But the well-known teenager survived and in 1955, after his recovery, he graduated from Greenwood High School and was offered a partial scholarship to study theater at Jackson State College.

Morgan had a decision to make. He loved acting, but seeing all those movies and daydreaming about fighter jets had made an impression. "I wanted to *fly*," he says.

So Morgan Freeman, the young romantic and gifted actor, joined the U.S. Air Force.

2

RUDE AWAKENINGS

Morgan Freeman was especially suited to narrate The Promised Land, *a five-hour Discovery Channel special on the northward migration of African Americans between 1942 and 1970, having taken part in the migration with his own family.*

MORGAN FREEMAN'S APTITUDE tests for the air force showed that he had the ability to be trained as a fighter pilot. Instead, he was assigned duty as a radar mechanic. "I ended up as a . . . radar technician because I was aced out," he explained in 1988. Although Freeman claims that racial prejudice was part of the reason he wasn't accepted as a pilot, he also acknowledges that he wasn't exactly a model soldier. "I called a horse's ass a horse's ass, even if it was wearin' brass," he declared bluntly. "The whole thing in the service, you're supposed to look down. Never could do that."

Freeman also concedes that being a victim of racism is not an excuse. "That's just something to overcome," he says. Nor does he feel that it has prevented him from achieving any of his goals. "Whatever obstacles you run into, it's easy to say 'You know, they wouldn't let me. I wanted to, I tried, but I'm black so. . . .' It's the easiest copout. So it's a little more difficult! Boy! So what? Who's got it easy?" he told a *USA Today* interviewer in 1997. Freeman also believes that racism goes both ways: "If I constantly tell you that you're against me, pretty soon you're going to say 'I don't want to get near this guy.'"

Freeman maintains that one of the difficulties he had with succeeding in the air force was his unwillingness to conform to rules. "I was a good radar mechanic, but a bad soldier," he recalled in an interview at the start of his acting career. He dislikes discussing his years in the air force at San Bernardino, California, and he once snapped, "I learned that the military is the place for people who don't want to think for themselves."

Despite his seeming bitterness, Freeman tells of one incident that illustrates his resistance to military discipline:

> [The technical sergeant] has these boxes of high-voltage diodes for working radar. He said, "You want to take these boxes up to the sixth tower radar dome?" And I said "no." And this guy looked at me. "No? No?! What do you mean, 'no'?" I said, "I mean, no, I don't *want* to take this damn box up to the sixth tower. You want me to take it up there, you *tell* me! You're *asking* me." That's not conducive to getting along in the military.

Nevertheless, racial discrimination in the U.S. armed forces during the 1950s was not a figment of Morgan Freeman's imagination. Despite the laudable World War II record of the famous Tuskegee Airmen and the earlier career of Eugene Jacques Bullard (a black pilot who flew in World War I with the Lafayette Escadrille), the air force in the 1950s had barely begun to integrate its troops. President Harry Truman had ordered all U.S. armed forces to integrate in 1948, but even though his orders were implemented more quickly in the air force and navy than in other branches of the services, many air force officers and servicemen still held their own prejudices toward blacks. Under such circumstances, a change in behavior and attitude was slow in coming. As a result, very few blacks were permitted to become fighter pilots in the 1950s.

Freeman now feels that his own desire to be a fighter pilot was misplaced. "I was a child of the war propaganda films, and I had a lot of fantasies," he told the *Washington Post*. Once he really thought about what a jet plane was for and what a fighter pilot's job

entailed, he decided it wasn't a career he wanted to pursue after all. Why did he ever think of military piloting as his vocation?

> I'm just a born romantic, and if you're romantic, the military just beckons. They sell it so wonderfully in the movies, on TV: "Be all that you can be." *Man!* But I didn't think at the time about what a soldier's real true calling is. It isn't really real until you've got a loaded gun and an enemy in front of you, or the potential for that. There are no shades of gray anywhere.

After Freeman sat in the cockpit of a T-33 jet trainer for a few minutes, he realized that his day-dreams and vivid imagination were more thrilling than real life. "Sitting there thinking 'This is a killing machine and there's no other reason to be in it than to kill,' that just wiped [those fantasies]

Like other African Americans who served in the U.S. military, Morgan Freeman was a victim of discrimination. Black soldiers had a proud history of service dating back to the Revolutionary War, yet they were often forced to fight in segregated units with inferior training and equipment before President Harry S Truman ordered the U.S. military to desegregate in 1948. This group of black pilot-heroes of World War II is known as the Tuskegee Airmen after the school at which they studied. They paved the way for racial equality in the military a decade before Freeman's enlistment.

away," says Freeman. He admitted to himself that what he really wanted to do was "*pretend* to fly, with the camera sitting right over there, clouds in the background," as he described it in 1986. If the movies had given him the desire to be a fighter pilot, Morgan Freeman decided, then he'd "fly" in the movies instead.

Some time after his discharge from the air force in 1959, Morgan went to Los Angeles, looked up the address of Paramount Studios, and presented himself there. "I thought you could go out there and say, 'I'm here!'" he laughed. Once again, Freeman spent a few months eating very little. He didn't have a car, and he had almost no money, so he walked everywhere. He relied on friends for a good meal every now and then, but eventually "pride wouldn't let me keep going [to their homes for food]," he says. "I got to where I didn't eat anything but milk and raw eggs. I'd beat 'em up in a glass, and that'd be a meal."

Finally, in May 1961, Morgan landed a job at Los Angeles City College as a transcript clerk, and he enrolled in acting, diction, and voice classes. "I was walkin' in tall cotton!" he recalls excitedly. He and his classmates taped their voices at the beginning of the semester and again at the end, and both Morgan and his fellow students were amazed by the improvement in his diction. Freeman was inspired to work even harder. "By the time I got out of there, I was really rounding out the ovals and hitting the final consonants and sounding real good," he says.

When his courses were over, Freeman drove cross-country to New York City to try out his newly honed acting skills. "I spent five months in New York," he said years later, "and all that happened was I joined the Negro Actors Guild, for [a fee of] ten dollars." He worked briefly as a telegrapher, but his acting career wasn't progressing as he'd hoped. Before long, he headed back to the West Coast—this time to San Francisco.

There, Freeman joined a repertory company called the Opera Ring. He was first cast as the street singer in Bertolt Brecht and Kurt Weill's *Threepenny Opera*, and he received his first review, in the *San Francisco Chronicle*. Years later, he still remembered every word of the review. "It went like this," he says, "'Morgan Freeman proclaims the return of the celebrated crook with an appropriate blend of awe, respect, wry humor, and barely perceptible sadness.'" But when Freeman refused to play an American Indian in a play called *Little Mary Sunshine*, he lost his job with the Opera Ring. He had objected to the ending of the script in which the "reformed" Native American character ends up waving an American flag. "You gonna tell me an Indian is gonna do *that*?" he demanded at the time.

Around this time one of Morgan's teachers advised him to take dance classes to make himself more marketable as a performer. Doing so was a severe financial hardship, but he took the advice. Freeman spent a lot of time trying to make enough money to pay for his dance classes and still afford food and a place to live. He took a variety of odd jobs—washing cars, selling ads for a black-run magazine, working at the post office. "I bummed a lot and lived on quarter-pound Baby Ruths [candy bars] for dinner," he remembers. When a dance teacher saw the thin young man eating a candy bar one day and guessed that it was his dinner, she gave him a scholarship. After a few years of struggle in San Francisco, Freeman returned to New York City, where he would live until 1990.

Once he was back east, Freeman landed a part as a

dancer at the 1964 World's Fair. But after that job, he "couldn't get *nuthin'*, and I ended up as a counterman at Nedick's in Penn Station" selling hot dogs and drinks. But the man who had quit a badly needed acting job in San Francisco on a matter of principle wasn't likely to take anyone's guff:

> I was taking home $49.04 for several nine-hour days a week, and my [boss] says to me "We have a no-tipping policy here." "What if they leave a tip and walk away?" I asked. "Ring it up as a sale," the man says. I did over a hundred dollars a week out of that place. See, if you tell me you're going to exploit me, I'm free to exploit you back.

In 1966, Freeman got a job as an understudy and chorus member with a touring show called *The Royal Hunt of the Sun*. He realized his career had been getting off-track—he was now dancing, but not acting. But then a lead actor collapsed on stage, and Morgan assumed his role. It was the break he had been waiting for. "Acting! That's what I was supposed to be doing," he says. "After that, my acting career just took off."

In 1967, Freeman landed a role in George Tabori's *The Niggerlovers*, an off-Broadway production at the Orpheum Theatre in New York City. The work was actually two one-act plays called *The Demonstration* and *Man and Dog*, and Freeman played the role of Creampuff in both plays. Through a fellow actor, Stacy Keach, Freeman got in touch with agent Jeff Hunter, who got him cast that same year as Rudolph in an all-black version of the musical *Hello, Dolly!* starring the legendary performers Pearl Bailey and Cab Calloway.

That summer, Freeman performed in *A Taste of Honey* at summer stock theater in Stowe, Vermont. "I became another person that year," he recalls. He was

After leaving the military, Freeman aimed to become an actor but found it difficult to get parts. One of his earliest performing opportunities was as a dancer at the 1964 World's Fair, held in New York City.

introduced to a pastime that has become a passion for him and that rivals even his acting career—sailing. And in October 1967, Freeman married Jeanette Adair Bradshaw. He adopted Jeanette's daughter, Deena; the couple later had another daughter whom they named Morgana.

The acting jobs kept coming. In 1969 alone, Freeman landed roles in three plays in three different cities: as Boston Baboon in Bertolt Brecht's *In the Jungle of Cities* in Boston, Massachusetts; as the sergeant in George Farquhar's *The Recruiting Officer* in Philadelphia, Pennsylvania; and as Foxtrot in Bruce Jay Friedman's *Scuba Duba* in the New Theatre in New York City. During the 1969–70 season, he performed in Gordon Watkins's *Caught in the Middle*, and he starred in the short-lived *Purlie* at the American National Theatre and Academy (ANTA). The following year, Freeman played Afro in a film called *Who Says I Can't Ride a Rainbow?* (also known as *Barney*).

The same year, Morgan Freeman also landed a role on a children's TV show that would influence a whole generation: *The Electric Company*. The program, produced by the Children's Television Workshop, was an educational production for children and adults who were just learning to read. Freeman played the hip, urbane Easy Reader, a role for which, to his chagrin, he is still often remembered.

Freeman was delighted to have regular work. The show paid him the princely sum of about $17,000 a year. It was a windfall for an actor with a family to support.

But it wasn't just the money that was appealing. "The vibes were good, [the cast was like] a family, and watching [costar] Bill Cosby all the time was something else," Freeman recalls. Playing Easy Reader was a regular 9-to-5 job for four months of each year, and it allowed Freeman to continue working in live theater the rest of the year. The schedule, the steady income, and an acting job in public television—Morgan Freeman began to believe that he was finally on the way to reaching his goal.

3

GETTING A TOEHOLD

— ❧ —

ALTHOUGH THE IMMENSELY popular *Electric Company* provided steady work and recognition, after five years the job began to wear on Morgan Freeman. He felt restless and frustrated in a role that was not expanding or offering him a chance at broader recognition. "You tell yourself, 'this is absolutely the last year I'm going to do this,'" Morgan said in a 1989 *New York Times* interview. After so long, he said, "I could hardly stand to get up in the morning and go to work."

Frustrated with his job but unwilling to give up a steady income, Freeman began to drink heavily. He felt trapped by his success as Easy Reader. "I was developing ulcers . . . and my first marriage started to crumble over the fact that I was doing something I didn't want to do anymore," he says. Years later, Freeman described how his alcohol abuse began:

Freeman was beginning to make his mark in theater when he was cast in the title role of the New York Shakespeare Festival production of Coriolanus *(1978). "From the moment he stepped onstage, Freeman's Coriolanus was a creature of awe," one critic raved.*

You start off going to lunch and having a martini, and then you have two martinis because you can do it, and then you go home and have two or three scotches because you can do it. But next thing I knew I was going through two or three quarts of whiskey a week. . . . I remember waking up once in my doorway, where I had fallen down. And I lay there thinking, "You're lying face down, drunk, and this will never do." And so I quit drinking.

Not long after, *The Electric Company* ceased production. "I'm afraid if it hadn't, I never would have left," Freeman says now. Although he believes that working on *The Electric Company* was a good experience for him and that the show was of high quality, Freeman is dismayed when fans of the show—many of whom are now parents—recognize him as Easy Reader. It makes him feel old. After all, he argues, he played that role decades ago. "It was a good show, a really good ensemble company, it really was, and I watched it sometimes long after I'd done it and walked away from it," he maintains. "But . . . I walk down the street and it's 'Hello, Easy Reader!' It's an ego problem—I'm an actor and I don't want to be Easy Reader forever!"

In 1972, while Freeman was still with *The Electric Company,* he took the role of Nate in *Gettin' It Together,* written by a young man named Richard Wesley. The play was one of four one-acts performed together as *Black Visions* by the New York Shakespeare Festival at the Public Theatre in New York. Freeman was highly impressed with the script: "I couldn't believe that this young guy in his twenties had written it. I wanted to *know* when he wrote something else."

Three years would pass before Freeman appeared onstage again, this time as Sisyphus in *Sisyphus and the Blue-Eyed Cyclops* (1975) in the off-off-Broadway Martinique Theatre. Two years later, he played Sampson in *Cockfight* by Elaine Jackson, at the American Place Theatre. Not until the spring of 1978 did Freeman have an opportunity to perform in another work by Richard Wesley. He was cast as Zeke in a Broadway production of *The Mighty Gents,* the story of the adult struggles of four former gang members in Newark, New Jersey.

Freeman auditioned for three parts—that of a father, Braxton the crook, and Zeke the wino (a derogatory term for an alcoholic who drinks wine). "I was given my choice of Braxton or Zeke and took

Zeke, and that was a challenge," he says. "It was something that was totally not me—an old man, a failure, a wino."

Freeman learned how to create such a character not only by studying the dialogue of the script but also from other actors he had watched carefully and from people he'd observed on the streets—and a bit of his own experience:

The cast of the children's public television program The Electric Company, *with Freeman, who played Easy Reader, at lower right. He was a member of the highly-regarded ensemble for five years, until the show ceased production.*

I had always watched [actor] Gig Young play drunks in the movies, and I understood that when a drunk slurs his words it is not because of sloppiness but because he is trying so hard to enunciate properly. His intensity *flattens* his words. I watched a [character that] Richard Pryor does, and I watched [people] on Broadway. . . . I recalled two long conversations I'd had with [alcoholics], in Greenwich Village and out in San Francisco.

To play Zeke, Freeman recalled an elderly and homeless alcoholic he'd once seen who had a trembling hand. "I worked on the look that comes into a man's eyes when he asks for a dime and is refused," he said. "The right voice and speech came more slowly. I tried to get across the feeling of where the voice had been by the time it was burnt out."

Freeman's performance, acclaimed by critics, was a breakthrough for him. He earned a prestigious Tony nomination, a Drama Desk Award for Outstanding Featured Actor in a Play, and the Clarence Derwent Award for Best Newcomer. (By this time the "newcomer," of course, was 40 years old and had been acting for roughly half of his life.) The *New York Times* called Freeman's performance "spectacular," and other reviewers were even more enthusiastic. "Freeman, eyes stricken with terror at his death-in-life, limbs twanging like a broken harp of flesh, face encrusted with dried-up hope, voice croaking like a buzzard on his own carrion, paints a shattering portrait of ultimate despair," reviewer Jack Kroll said in *Newsweek* magazine.

Despite excellent reviews, however, the play closed after only nine performances. Freeman was devastated. "I took it to heart," he told a *Washington Post* interviewer more than 10 years later. "I thought I was ready and here it came. But the play closed in a week and it sort of faded away." What disturbed Freeman most was that he felt the play's integrity had been compromised by its arrival on Broadway. "When they move something to Broadway . . . they want to Broadwayize it. If it's a nice, heavy, long piece of drama, they're gonna water it down so it fits this medium [he points to a television], which is what Broadway aspires to." Freeman's early experience taught him that awards and excellent reviews do not always equal success. Since then he has remained "decidedly indifferent" about reviews of his work, whether positive or negative.

He also learned that it isn't enough to admire other performers who have achieved a higher level of success than you have. A good actor aspires to improve himself and reach or exceed the level of excellence he admires. In October 1978, a few months after *The Mighty Gents* closed, Freeman appeared with famed actor José Ferrer in the play *White Pelicans*, a drama about two prospectors trying to return home after a luckless attempt to strike it rich. Once again, Freeman had a short run—the play closed after two weeks—but he learned another valuable lesson. "I was looking up to [José Ferrer]," Freeman says. "Finally he said, 'We're not going to be able to work together if you don't get one more rung up on the ladder.' You have to keep a level playing field [with fellow actors]," Freeman concluded, to create a successful performance.

In 1979 Freeman landed a supporting role in *Julius Caesar* with the New York Shakespeare Festival. His work was so well received that he got an even bigger part—the title role in Shakespeare's *Coriolanus*, also at the New York Shakespeare Festival. "From the moment he stepped onstage," said one journalist, "Freeman's Coriolanus was a creature of awe, a battle-scarred warrior who was still a snob, who couldn't stand the stink of the mob, who wouldn't follow custom and go among the people to display his wounds."

Freeman himself aptly described the character's nature: "This man is *bad*. He doesn't take *no* [grief] from *no*body at *no* time." The actor received an Obie award both for this performance and for that of the

In 1980, Freeman won his second Obie Award for his performance as the chaplain in Bertolt Brecht's Mother Courage and Her Children. *Freeman is pictured in the center; at right is Gloria Foster, who played the title role.*

chaplain in the 1980 production of Bertolt Brecht's *Mother Courage and Her Children*.

While Freeman's career seemed to be taking a positive turn, his personal life was not. After years of struggling, he and his wife, Jeanette, divorced in 1979. They had been married 12 years. Freeman threw himself into his work, appearing not only in *Mother Courage* but also in a TV movie called *Hollow Image*, and then in the 1980 film *Brubaker*, directed by actor Robert Redford, who also had the title role.

Brubaker is the tale of a reformist prison warden who tries to establish a policy of more humane treatment of inmates. Freeman plays a ferocious and desperate death-row convict who is driven nearly insane by the conditions of his confinement and tries to strangle an inmate. Freeman's character demands that his cell be painted and given a window. In an attempt to appease him, the warden agrees to make the changes and gets the convict to return to his cell. Under his leadership, death-row inmates are allowed out of their cells once a day.

For Morgan Freeman, 1980 was a year for prison films. He appeared in *Attica*, a powerful TV movie based on the true story of the violent inmate revolt at the New York state penitentiary in 1971. After a few small movie roles in 1981, Freeman returned to the stage. At the Dallas Shakespeare Festival, he first performed as the Duke of Florence in *All's Well That Ends Well* and then took the title role in *Othello*. Despite the prestige of having a starring role in one of Shakespeare's finest dramas, however, Morgan Freeman was disappointed with the experience. "I was lousy in *Othello*," Freeman admitted to a reporter in 1988. Part of the reason for his difficulty, he claims, is that Shakespeare wrote *Othello* as though he were a white man with black skin, not as a real black man, whose culture and experiences were alien to the playwright.

By the end of 1982, Freeman was back in New York, where he had another minor stage role and landed a job as architect Roy Bingham on the daytime soap opera *Another World*. His major accomplishment in this job, he remarked years later, was in not letting the writers name his character "George Washington Jones" or a similarly stereotypical black name. Freeman's character appeared on the program sporadically until 1984. During breaks from shooting, he also appeared in a short-lived off-Broadway play called *Buck*.

By this time Freeman had begun to develop a reputation among some directors as being difficult to work with, because he constantly challenged their conceptions of how his characters should be portrayed. Friends and observers believe that this

Morgan Freeman was frighteningly convincing as a death-row inmate in the 1980 movie Brubaker, *which starred Robert Redford (left) in the title role as a warden who wants to reform the prison.*

reputation was undeserved. "All he was doing was challenging the clichés and insensitivities that seemed to come with the roles he was being offered as a black actor," says interviewer Richard Harrington. Freeman has been unafraid to turn down roles—and is sometimes passed over for other roles—that seem to perpetuate stereotypes of black Americans. What happened, he said, is that he "started talking about race . . . with people who didn't want to deal with this stuff. That accounted for some dry spells." He describes one encounter with movie producers who were looking to sign him on for a project they were developing: "'Any other black people in this movie?' I asked them. They all looked at one another. 'We don't believe so,' they said. 'We never thought of it in racial terms.' Well, that was a lie right there— I mean, they were casting me as an orderly—and [I knew I didn't want the part]."

Freeman's friend Mel Boudrot, who is also an actor, believes that some people find the six-foot-two-inch Freeman intimidating. "He has a way of going for the essence of things, and knocking whatever else is floating around to the side," Boudrot says. "Add to that Morgan's attitude that 'color' shouldn't exist, his height—which he uses—[and] his tendency to [know when] you're scared of him," and you have quite a daunting figure. Boudrot and other friends of Freeman also worried that because age often determines who gets the biggest movie roles, Freeman was making it harder than necessary by being difficult about possible racial stereotypes.

Freeman did manage to find acting jobs and avoid ever serving hot dogs again as a career, but his life as an actor certainly was not easy. Good work was hard to come by, and although he had been nominated for—and had won—several prestigious acting awards, the job offers still didn't come pouring in. In fact, the life of an actor began wearing on him. Several times during this period he considered leaving the business entirely. What had once seemed like a promising career, a way of "taking flight," had begun to ground the 47-year-old Morgan Freeman.

4

TAXI DRIVING?

P ERHAPS IT WAS the combination of *Buck's* disappointing five-performance run and Morgan Freeman's marriage to costume designer Myrna Colley-Lee in 1983 that made the actor examine his life and what career he would ultimately pursue. He was so discouraged from years of trying to make it in theater and film that he seriously considered giving up acting for good and getting a taxi-driver's license.

Fortunately, actor-director Paul Newman found out that Freeman had been idle for some time. "He said, 'That's criminal,' and hired me," Freeman recalled in 1995. Working with Newman, he appeared in the film *Harry and Son* in 1984 and had a minor role later the same year in *Teachers*. A taxi-driving career, at least for the moment, was out.

Not long after, he received a phone call from Lee Breuer, who was directing a play called *The Gospel at Colonus*, based on the Oedipus cycle of ancient Greek drama. Breuer's project had an unusual twist, however: it was set in a modern Pentecostal church.

Freeman had never heard of Breuer, but when the director explained his idea and told Freeman why he planned to use American gospel singers instead of classical music, the actor was sold. "Then he tells me, 'I need a star to glue it all together,'" Freeman recalls, "and I say 'I'm no star,' and he says 'Well, I'm going to make you [one].' Me? A star? I got two words for you: Hah. Hah."

"Morgan, this is gonna knock 'em dead," Freeman told himself upon completing his first run-through of The Gospel at Colonus. *The actor was right: the production won numerous awards, toured Europe and the United States, and opened on Broadway in 1988. Freeman himself netted his third Obie Award with his powerful performance, which also gave new life to his flagging career.*

43

Breuer wanted Freeman for the role of the preacher, a main character. Freeman was still doubtful, until he heard some of the music for the production and it gave him goosebumps. So he signed on. And the goosebumps continued up to his first run-through in Minneapolis, Minnesota:

> When I stepped onstage . . . and I spoke the first words [in a deep, ringing voice], "Think no longer that you are in command here," when I said that first line and heard the members of the choir going "Amen!" behind me, I said to myself, "Morgan, this is gonna knock 'em dead." And then that joyous music broke out, and all that incredible singin', and all kinds of Jesus noises goin' on, it just wrung me. . . . I've been in a lotta shows in my life, and I've thought a lot of 'em were pretty good, but this is a *masterpiece.*
>
> I wanted to call everyone, right then. I wanted to get on the phone and tell everyone I know, "*Man, this is what theater is all about.*"

The play's stunning musical score was only one of the reasons Freeman enjoyed performing in *The Gospel at Colonus.* He was also allowed a measure of creative input. "I work best when I feel I can have ideas and express them," the actor says. "Sometimes I get in trouble when I open my big mouth, but it can be a very creative part of the process when people are receptive." For example, Freeman asked Breuer to limit the audience's applause so that the momentum of the work would not be interrupted. "You let the audience applaud every time they want to, we're talking 'bout swollen hands—and by intermission," he playfully told an interviewer in 1988. For his part, Breuer declared that he considered Freeman his "assistant director." He added:

> He has the ability to know what the moment demands. He added professionalism without adding slickness. He provided a plumb line to direct and vital contact with the audience. . . . We had a little conversation early on. It was the best piece of directing I ever gave him. "You are no longer a character actor," I told him. "You've got

it all to become a star. And to do this part right, you have to *think* of yourself as a star. You have to feel that no one else onstage is worth looking at." I think he thought of himself as a star for the first time. He should—everybody else does.

The Gospel at Colonus was immensely popular and critically acclaimed. For his performance, Freeman won another Obie award. The show toured Europe and the United States for several years before moving to Broadway in 1988, with Freeman again in the lead role. Freeman explained why he thought the production struck such a strong chord in its audiences: "People don't usually go to the theater expecting spiritual uplift or redemption," he said, "but this show gives them something they've been missing that they don't even *know* they've been missing, the experience of soul."

After a number of small roles, including parts in the 1985 films *Marie* and *That Was Then, This Is Now* and the TV movies *The Atlanta Child Murders* (1985) and *Resting Place* (1986), Freeman landed the role of a pimp named Fast Black in the 1987 film *Street Smart*, which also starred Christopher Reeve and Kathy Baker.

Although it may seem surprising that Freeman, who has always been very selective about the roles he accepts, would be eager to portray such a seemingly stereotypical character, he had no intentions of playing Fast Black as a typical ghetto bad guy. Instead he transformed the sparsely written role into a memorable and frighteningly powerful character, "the kind of guy who can hold a gun to your throat, then slowly smile, pat you on the cheek, and say 'Come on, I'll buy you a cuppa coffee,'" *Time* magazine wrote in 1990. "Freeman play[s] a man so tautly in control he could snap into psychosis at any second, a man, most of all, who knows that a large part of being a successful pimp is being a gifted actor," the interviewer continued.

Freeman was determined to play Fast Black as a

real, three-dimensional man. "What is a pimp?" he asked his interviewer while walking down 42nd Street in New York. "Can you walk along here and pick one out? The way they usually play 'em in movies, you can. That's just a caricature. No one I've ever seen in movies has done a person I *know*." When asked how he researches a role like this, Freeman declares that he simply goes with what he feels. "It doesn't do me any good to intellectualize about it."

So if talking about the role didn't help, how did he find out how to play a character who is completely alien to him? Freeman says that he "started putting the character in place" after he began searching for the kind of clothes he thought the man might wear. Once he felt that he knew who Fast Black was, Freeman became so immersed in the character that it was often difficult for him to shake it off.

In one particularly harrowing scene, Fast Black holds a pair of scissors to the face of one of his "girls," Punchy (Kathy Baker). It is "one of the most chilling scenes in movie history," said one reviewer. "I'm gonna take one eye. Just one," says Fast Black. "You have to tell me which one—right or left?" he says, as he switches the scissors back and forth. Baker remembers shooting the scene and the intensity of Freeman's performance: "The people who were watching us were so frightened, they were standing flat against the walls," she said. "But I trusted Morgan so much, I could give myself over to it completely. Kathy Baker wasn't afraid, so I was free to let the character be totally scared out of her mind."

Similarly, Jerry Schatzberg, the director, remarked that Freeman often seemed to remain in character even when not shooting a scene. Even though it wasn't Freeman's nature to do so, he was so good at playing his character that he "used to frighten the crew, snapping at them," Schatzberg remembers. "I finally had to tell him to cool it," the director says.

Once again, the actor thrived in an atmosphere

*In 1985, Freeman took a small
role in the film* That Was
Then, This Is Now; *he also
acted in a television movie called*
The Atlanta Child Murders.

where his suggestions were taken seriously. Baker
remembers that while they were shooting the
famous "scissors scene," Morgan insisted that the
cameras focus not on his face, but on Baker's. "'No,
no, this isn't my scene, this is Kathy's scene,' [Morgan
said], and he reached out and put his hand over my
face—'*This* is where it's happening'—and that's the
way it is in the film. How many actors would do
that?" she asks.

The influential film critic Pauline Kael, writing
for *New Yorker* magazine, began her review of *Street
Smart* with a question—"Is Morgan Freeman the

"I'm gonna take one eye. . . . You have to tell me which one," pimp Fast Black (Freeman) tells prostitute Punchy (Kathy Baker) in this scene from 1987's Street Smart that a reviewer later called "one of the most chilling scenes in movie history." Morgan's taut performance earned him an Oscar nomination for Best Supporting Actor.

greatest American actor?"—and concluded that he was. Freeman's riveting portrayal earned him an Academy Award nomination for Best Supporting Actor. But before the winners were even announced, Freeman insisted that he didn't want the award. "Can't use it," he remarked to an interviewer. He explained why:

Character actors only get but so many chances to work. *Black* character actors have it even harder—we have 95 percent unemployment! I'm in the top five percent of my field. . . . Now if I won the Academy Award, I might not be able to accept among the scripts that I *do* want, because of the scale of pay. In other words, [say] there's a [less prestigious] part I like but they won't offer it to me, or I won't be able to take it, because [now I'm an award-winner and] the money's too low. . . . Then you find yourself doing "great man" parts, roles meant to make everyone feel reassured.

But Morgan Freeman has never been one to play it safe. The roles he's chosen in his long career reflect great social, economic, and racial differences among people. "You have to understand," a friend of Morgan's remarks, "'safe' roles for blacks are cops, social workers, athletes, musicians. Morgan has always been all over the lot."

Freeman didn't win that Oscar he claimed not to want, but he did earn other accolades for his performance in *Street Smart*, including awards from the New York Film Critics Circle, the Los Angeles Film Critics, the National Society of Film Critics, and a nomination for a Golden Globe Award. What makes this accomplishment even more remarkable is that the film itself lasted only a few weeks in movie theaters before being pulled.

The same year that Freeman starred in *Street Smart*, he heard of a play called *Driving Miss Daisy* that was being produced off-Broadway by Playwrights Horizons. It "sounded real interesting," Morgan recalls, and he wondered who he had to see to get involved in it. "A couple of months later, I get a call. Would I be interested in doing a play at Playwrights Horizons? Turns out it's the same play. Damn right I'm interested!" Freeman laughs.

Although Freeman loved the script, he worried that the role of Hoke Colburn, a gentle but strong-minded chauffeur for an elderly white woman, was too old for him to play. But when the directors explained that they preferred "quality rather than age," Freeman says that his head "explode[d] four or five times its normal size." He was even more delighted to hear that his costar in the title role was veteran actress Dana Ivey.

The play was a huge hit, landing Freeman his fourth Obie Award. When the play was made into a film, Morgan Freeman again played Hoke, with Jessica Tandy as Daisy and Dan Ackroyd as her worrisome son, Boolie.

Freeman's first starring role was in the 1988 film Lean on Me, *based on the true story of Joe Clark, the principal of an inner-city high school who inspired his students to improve their lives. Clark was famous for walking through the halls wielding a baseball bat and dealing quickly and effectively with trouble-makers, drug dealers, and criminals who bothered students in his school.*

Freeman's portrayal of Hoke Colburn was so vastly different from his Fast Black character that *Miss Daisy* playwright Alfred Uhry declared that had he seen the actor in *Street Smart*, he would never have believed Freeman could play the chauffeur role. But Freeman maintains that Fast Black and Hoke are both "just providing services in an imperfect society. Yeah, they'd've dug what the other guy was up to. That's just obvious, isn't it?"

Reviewers praised Freeman for making Hoke gentle without being subservient. "The character emerges as a natural aristocrat, who just happened to be born on the wrong side of the tracks," wrote David Richards of the *Washington Post*. Such lauda-tory reviews in nationally popular publications cemented Freeman's reputation as a fine stage actor.

While the stage run of *Driving Miss Daisy* was still

in progress, Freeman also played a counselor named Craig in the 1988 film *Clean and Sober,* which also starred Michael Keaton and Kathy Baker. And then, just as *Miss Daisy* was ending, he landed his first starring film role in the movie *Lean on Me.* Having won the role was especially rewarding to Freeman, because among the other actors considered for the role had been his screen idol, Sidney Poitier.

By the late 1980s, Freeman believes, "Things were [staying] together long enough that I knew I might stay glued for a while. Every year I found that I was still working and still going." Fortunately for Morgan Freeman and his fans, he had completely ruled out a career as a taxi driver.

5

THE FUN BEGINS

❧

The 1989 movie Glory made public the little-known story of the African Americans who served their country honorably during the Civil War, despite segregation and other hardships. "This is a moment in history that had been excised, forgotten. . . . To bring that back where it belongs . . . is a wonderful undertaking," Morgan Freeman said of the film. For his performance as Union Army Sergeant John Rawlins, Freeman won a Golden Globe Award and was nominated for an Oscar.

MORGAN FREEMAN KNOWS from long experience that glorious reviews and award nominations may be signs of fame and fortune, but they are fleeting. Freeman also knows that although conditions in the film industry have improved, the availability of good roles for most minority men and women remains limited. With the release of director Spike Lee's film *She's Gotta Have It* in 1986, the playing field for black film professionals began to show signs of evening up. Still, there are very few blacks and other minorities working in the studio "system."

Except for filmmaker Oliver Micheaux, whose film career spanned the 1920s, 1930s, and 1940s, there were no black producers in Hollywood as a rule. Talented actors such as Stepin Fetchit (the first black to receive star billing), Hattie McDaniel (the first black, male or female, to win an Oscar), and Bill "Bojangles" Robinson were largely relegated to playing stereotyped roles in which they were always subservient to whites. One frequently cited exception to this rule during the late 1940s and the 1950s was the elegant actor Sidney Poitier. Morgan Freeman viewed Poitier as a role model partly because he played non-stereotypical roles in major films. Encouraged by Poitier's success, Freeman reasoned that there must also be "room in Hollywood" for an actor like him.

Freeman with one of the actors he most admires, Sidney Poitier. In the 1940s and 1950s, Poitier was one of the few African-American actors able to play non-stereotypical movie roles.

By the late 1960s, however, in the midst of the civil rights and black power movements, the type of roles Poitier played were criticized by some blacks for being "sterile" or "middle-class." Most black movie-goers wanted to see someone more like themselves on screen, more earthy, perhaps even more imperfect characters than those Poitier was known for.

In 1969, Gordon Parks Sr. became the first black director of a major studio film with the release of

The Learning Tree for Warner Bros. Studios. Parks believes that breaking the racial barrier in his field was the result of just a few people in powerful positions making a commitment to do so. The rest of the industry had no choice but to follow suit.

A few years after *The Learning Tree* was released, Melvin Van Peebles managed to raise enough money to produce the 1971 release *Sweet Sweetback's Baad Asssss Song*. According to author Jesse Algeron Rhines in the 1996 book *Black Film/White Money*, Van Peebles's film singlehandedly "changed the course of African-American film production and the depiction of African Americans on screen." But the change was hardly positive. Along with the films *Shaft* (1971, directed by Parks) and *Superfly* (1972, directed by Parks's son Gordon Parks Jr.), *Sweet Sweetback* ushered in the era of "blaxploitation" films. The term, coined by the industry publication *Variety*, refers to the films of that period that portray blacks as promiscuous criminals or drug pushers, some of the very stereotypes that blacks were working to abolish. Except for these three films, most "blaxploitation" movies were written, directed, and distributed by whites, whom many accused of exploiting their audiences' wish to see black stars on the big screen. These films still represented a negative view of blacks—albeit one that was popular among young blacks because of its extremism.

After a time, actors like Poitier (still a powerful influence in Hollywood), Harry Belafonte, Bill Cosby, and Ossie Davis, and enterprises such as the black-owned distribution companies TAM and Cinematics International, brought a return to filmmaking that portrayed blacks in realistic but positive ways.

On the advice of his agent, Jeff Hunter from William Morris, Morgan Freeman avoided taking roles in blaxploitation films. Not until the mid-1980s did he break into the film industry in a big way—and by then, Hollywood had changed quite a bit.

The industry had discovered the "blockbuster" film. This was the age of *Star Wars*, *Jaws*, and the Indiana Jones movies. Instead of targeting modestly budgeted films to select audiences, Hollywood began investing huge amounts of money in adventures that were calculated to have the broadest possible audience appeal. Once again, however, black actors, directors, and other film professionals found themselves largely ignored by Hollywood. Aside from Richard Pryor and Eddie Murphy, who became superstars that could pull in a sizeable black audience, the beginning of the blockbuster era offered few new opportunities for blacks. Critics say that studio executives operate on the assumption that most audiences are predominantly white and will only watch movies about other whites. This unproven belief, they argue, is what causes studios to ignore black actors and black-themed screenplays.

Others argue that it is not racism but economics that perpetuates the problem. Yaphet Kotto, who has held significant roles in Hollywood-produced films (including the 1979 movie *Alien*), is among them. "People want to be involved in fifteen- to twenty-million-dollar movies, and they want their returns guaranteed," Kotto maintains. "So they go for the [Robert] Redfords, the [Sean] Connerys, the [Marlon] Brandos. . . . If they ever scale their expectations down and return to modest, low-budget films, they might just turn to me."

Morgan Freeman's view of the situation is a bit more personal. The shortage of black roles in major pictures, he says, stems from the simple fact that most screenwriters are white, and "they write about what they know." He continues, "I imagine that if I wrote, I would write about black people, so there's no reason to hold a pistol to a white writer's head and say, 'Write about black people.' . . . It's not the white writers' responsibility. You want material, write it," he says bluntly. So in 1987, when Freeman had the opportunity to act in a film produced by a major studio, he jumped at it. And for him, the catch was his age, not his race.

The stage version of *Driving Miss Daisy* was an unlikely play to be made into a box-office hit. Its set and dialogue were sparse, it ran only 90 minutes, and only three characters (Dana Ivey as Daisy, Ray Gill as Boolie, and Morgan Freeman as Hoke Colburn) carried the play. But after two years as a stage production, a film project began to take shape. Director Bruce Beresford saw the play and went backstage to congratulate Freeman, but he was somewhat hesitant about signing Freeman for the film version. By this time, the film role of Miss Daisy had already been given to Jessica Tandy, a fine stage actress with a long and distinguished career—and a few decades on Freeman. Freeman remembers the conversation that ensued: "[Your performance is] great, but then, you're a bit young," said Beresford. "What do you mean I'm a bit young?" Freeman asked. "Did you believe me when you were out there?" "Yeah, I believed you," Beresford said. "So what's the problem?" Freeman asked. "You're a bit young." Freeman completes the story in a burst of laughter.

His age notwithstanding, Freeman got the role. Beresford later remarked, "I think Morgan could do almost anything. I think he and Robert Duvall [who has appeared in such movies as *The Apostle* and *Phenomenon*] are the two most skillful actors I have ever worked with in my life. Technically, they have enormous resources."

Not surprisingly, some black film critics viewed Morgan Freeman's role in *Driving Miss Daisy* as perpetuating the stereotypical role of blacks as servants to whites. Though the movie was highly successful,

Freeman translated his stage popularity to the screen in the 1989 hit movie version of Driving Miss Daisy.

its name became the catch-phrase for the kind of roles that many black actors and actresses refuse to play. This concept didn't occur to Freeman himself, he says, until white audience members began "flocking" to see him after stage performances "talking about how they're from the South and how it reminds them of family." He began to wonder whether the nostalgia his character evoked was also a desire to return to an age of extreme racial inequality. But when he asked his black friends what they thought, they responded in the same way: that the movie portrays "a wonderful relationship between two people. They'd say 'My grandfather was just like that,' or 'It reminds me so much of my uncle.'" With that, Freeman stopped worrying about whether he was perpetuating a stereotype.

Whatever people thought of Hoke Colburn, no one questioned Freeman's brilliant performance, and few reviewers question Freeman's talents in general. The actor got his first crack at a lead role in a major motion picture with *Lean on Me*. The filming—completed the same year that *Driving Miss Daisy* appeared in theaters—was an unusual experience for Freeman. Not only was his character, Joe Clark, a real and living person, but he was also on the set during the shooting. Clark was a New Jersey teacher who became the principal of one of the state's worst schools and managed to turn it around with a tough, no-nonsense approach to discipline. Of his portrayal of Clark, Freeman says:

> I have my own voice, my own set of rhythms, and although I studied Joe—followed him around, watched him in action—still I'm dealing with a script and a set parameter and he's himself. When you hear him over the PA system, see how he does things and hear how he uses words, you absorb that. But after a while you pass that, and it's just a matter of realizing what your limitations are and why.

By now, Freeman was well on his way to establishing himself as a major "player" in Hollywood. He landed roles in two other films released in 1989: *Johnny Handsome* and *Glory*. Although *Johnny Handsome* was a box-office failure, the movie *Glory* blazed through theaters, earning four Academy Award nominations and winning three: Best Cinematography, Best Sound, and Best Supporting Actor (awarded to Freeman's costar Denzel Washington). *Glory* became Freeman's favorite project. He played the role of John Rawlins, a gravedigger who joins the 54th Massachusetts, the first black volunteer regular infantry unit in the Civil War. Rawlins is eventually promoted to sergeant, the highest possible rank for a black man at the time. The film also starred Washington, Jihmi Kennedy, André Braugher, and Matthew Broderick as Robert Gould Shaw, the youthful white commander of the 54th.

Freeman feels that *Glory* is one of the most important films ever made because it chronicles the true story of the black soldiers who fought for their own freedom in the Civil War. Without films like *Glory* and the 1997 film *Amistad*, Freeman reasons, few would be aware of the great sacrifices made to secure liberty for blacks in America. "Everybody involved in [*Glory*], I think, was very spiritually involved," Freeman said in a 1989 *New York Times* interview. "This is a moment in history that had been excised, forgotten about. To bring that back where it belongs, close to the heart, is a wonderful undertaking."

For his performances in 1989, including *Driving Miss Daisy* and *Glory*, Freeman won a Golden Globe Award, a Silver Berlin Bear, and an Oscar nomination. Freeman says he has learned to ignore the "noise"—his word for media coverage—about his work. He intends to keep himself firmly planted in reality, despite his breakthrough successes. "The press

come around and tell you that you're just the greatest thing since smoked sausage," he said in the *Times* interview that year. "You fill out your chest and walk around balancing your head as best you can. But none of that translates into something you can give your landlord or your grocer or your cleaner."

Freeman spent the summer of 1990 in an unusual version of Shakespeare's *The Taming of the Shrew*, staged in Central Park at the Delacorte Theater. The performance was part of director Joseph Papp's grand project—which he called Shakespeare in the Park—of introducing new audiences to the playwright's works. Freeman played Petruchio to Tracey Ullman's Katharina, and the action was set in an Old West frontier town rather than Elizabethan England.

In an unusual staging of Shakespeare's Taming of the Shrew, *Morgan Freeman plays an "Old West" Petruchio at the Shakespeare in the Park performances of 1990. He is pictured here with costar Tracy Ullman (Katharina).*

Also in 1990 came the release of the widely panned *Bonfire of the Vanities*, based on the best-selling book by Tom Wolfe. Freeman was Judge White, a no-nonsense, streetwise, and demanding urban judge who presides over the trial of a wealthy white man for the hit-and-run death of a poor black teenager. In one of the movie's most memorable scenes, White delivers a commonsense lecture to the rabid courtroom crowd: "Go home," he says, "and be decent to each other."

Freeman quickly recovered from *Bonfire's* box-office disaster the following year, when he appeared as Azeem in the popular *Robin Hood: Prince of Thieves*, starring Kevin Costner, Christian Slater, and Mary Elizabeth Mastrantonio. Azeem is a civilized Moor who finds England dangerous and inhospitable. The character was not in the original Robin Hood legend, but he adds a touch of the exotic to an otherwise predictable but action-filled tale.

With the 1992 release of the Clint Eastwood film *Unforgiven*, Freeman stepped outside tradition and played the role of a cowboy. *Unforgiven* is a dark, unusual western: there are no "good" or "bad" guys, and the film is perhaps the only one to portray women and minorities in the Old West in the balanced numbers that reflect what the American frontier was really like. *Unforgiven* earned nine Oscar nominations and netted four awards, including Best Picture, Best Director (Eastwood), and Best Supporting Actor (Gene Hackman). It also earned two Golden Globe Awards and a New York Film Critics Award. Freeman became so fond of westerns that he has been working on his own screenplay about that era in American history. One of his favorite figures is Bass Reeves, a black man who served for 32 years as a deputy U.S. marshal in the territory that is now Oklahoma.

A lesser-known movie, released the same year,

was *The Power of One*, a chronicle of an orphaned English boy living in South Africa during the 1940s who experiences prejudice from white Afrikaaners (South Africans of Dutch descent). The boy, named P. K., is befriended by a German pianist and a black boxing coach named Geel Piet (Freeman), who teaches him to box and to stand up for himself.

Freeman continued to explore apartheid—a policy of segregation and political and economic discrimination against blacks and other non-Europeans in South Africa—in his first directing project, *Bopha!*

For his role as Red in the 1994 film The Shawshank Redemption, *Freeman received Oscar and Golden Globe nominations. The film, which also starred Tim Robbins, was based on a short story by Stephen King.*

The movie starred Danny Glover as a police officer named Mikah and Alfre Woodard as his wife, Rosie. Mikah's carefully constructed view of the way the world "should" work is shattered by his son Zweli's rebellion against the racist white system. While not a box-office hit, the movie earned critical praise for Freeman, Glover, and Woodard.

Freeman returned to acting in the 1994 film *The Shawshank Redemption*, based on the Stephen King short story, "Rita Hayworth and the Shawshank Redemption." The movie featured Tim Robbins as the ambiguous Andy, a young banker convicted of murdering his wife and her lover. Freeman is the narrator, Red, also a convicted murderer and a "lifer" who befriends Andy and helps him adapt to prison life—and is rewarded for his effort. For his steady, graceful performance, Morgan Freeman earned best actor nominations for an Academy Award, a Golden Globe Award, and a Screen Actors Guild Award.

The honors were enough to make Hollywood finally take notice of Freeman's talents. The following year, he appeared in two major films: *Seven*, in which he played a brilliant detective who tracks a serial killer with a literary mind; and *Outbreak*, a fictional story about a highly infectious disease that spreads throughout northern California while a team of scientists races to discover an anti-serum.

Some critics blamed *Seven*'s intensity and graphic detail for scaring potential moviegoers away. For Freeman, however, the project offered a rare opportunity to step outside of himself and see his work from a viewer's perspective: "It's a coup, a major accomplishment if I can get far enough outside of me to watch me objectively," he said in an interview with *Filmweb*. "I managed it a couple of times—including the second viewing of *Seven*—but ordinarily it's too difficult. . . . When I was doing stage work I [was able to] look at myself strictly through the eyes of the audience. . . . Then you get into film and you can see yourself and all that stuff falls to pieces. You can just see your own little human weak self. That's what I see."

The 1996 films *Moll Flanders* with Robin Wright and *Chain Reaction* with Keanu Reeves slowed Freeman's momentum somewhat; neither film was a box-office success and reviews were tepid. He rebounded in 1997, however, with *Kiss the Girls*, based on a novel by James Patterson, and the long-awaited Steven Spielberg production *Amistad*.

Although Freeman's role in *Kiss the Girls* was that of a cop chasing down a serial killer—much like his role in *Seven*—moviegoers apparently were not bothered by the similarity. In its first two weeks, *Kiss the Girls* netted $28.5 million. The actor balks at the suggestion that it was a knockoff of *Seven*. "It's like comparing *Kiss the Girls* to a musical. . . . It's an insult to James Patterson, for one," Freeman told *Mr. Showbiz* in 1997. "The things that you put together are Morgan Freeman and cop, the things that I put together are character and plot."

One of Morgan Freeman's most critically acclaimed roles was that of a freed slave defending a group of Africans who escaped their chains and slaughtered their white captors while en route to America—and to slavery. Comparing *Amistad's* epic scope to that of the film *Schindler's List*, also directed by Stephen Spielberg, Freeman predicted that Amistad would be "one of the events of the decade." He was right: the film was a smashing success, and Freeman earned an Image Award for Best Supporting Actor from the National Association for the Advancement of Colored People (NAACP).

In addition to the increasing number of big studio productions that Freeman has participated in, he

Audiences flocked to the theaters to see Morgan Freeman play detective Alex Cross in the film version of James Patterson's novel Kiss the Girls. In its first two weeks of release, the film netted $28.5 million.

has also lent his smooth baritone voice to several documentaries: the acclaimed PBS series *The Civil War*, directed by Ken Burns (1990); the Rabbit Ears production *The Savior is Born* (1993); *Cosmic Voyage* in 1996; and *The Long Way Home*, an award-winning film about the creation of Israel, released in 1997. Freeman's voice is only one of his many assets. Critics praise his remarkable ability to "adopt" the appearance of each of his characters. Richard Harrington of the *Washington Post* declared that the actor has "a mobile face [that] lends itself to

[his] needs. . . . [It] can be warm and gregarious, stern and demanding, heroic, demeaning, stoic, sinister . . . reflect[ing] not only the range of emotion, but the range of Freeman's experiences."

It seems safe to say that after more than thirty years of professional acting, Morgan Freeman has finally made it to the "big time." Film audiences and fans expect—and receive—great performances from him. But what does Freeman want for himself?

6

INHABITING HIMSELF

— ❦ —

"**I** DON'T PONDER roles. I read the script, and learn the lines," Morgan Freeman announced in 1995. "And wear the costumes correctly, if possible," he added drolly. Freeman doesn't believe in "immersing" himself in his roles, as some other actors do. He finds that he can do very well without such techniques. The only acting classes Freeman ever had were those at Los Angeles City College in the 1960s, when he was just starting out in the business. His role models for acting (as opposed to his career in general) were white actors: Gary Cooper, Humphrey Bogart, and, later, James Cagney. "They go right at the role, and that's all they do. No personality [business]. I did most of my learning in my first play onstage from Stacy Keach, just watching him prepare," said Morgan in 1986.

Now, after three decades of acting professionally, the actor admits that his job has become easier: "I think I'm enough of a technician, as it were, not to have to 'plumb the depths of my soul,'" he told *USA Today* in December 1997. He does not do heavy research to prepare for his roles the way some actors do. "If you choose the role, you should choose it because it's going to be easy for you. . . . I want to be challenged, but I don't want to be stumped." Freeman believes that his job isn't so much a creative effort as it is an interpretation of a script:

Behind the camera: Morgan Freeman makes his directorial debut in the 1993 film Bopha! *The film, which explored apartheid in South Africa, earned critical praise for Freeman and its stars, Danny Glover and Alfre Woodard.*

I always have to have very strong input from someone else, who has done the creating. The writer creates; the person who has the idea and sits down and puts it on the blank piece of paper—that's the creator. . . . I certainly don't create character. I take that off the page. If I created the character, it would be the same person every time out.

When he was filming the movie *Outbreak* with costar Dustin Hoffman, Freeman recalls Hoffman, a meticulous researcher, offering to send him information to develop his character. "I told him it was not going to change my performance, and he found that very amusing. But it's not going to change. What I'm going to do is going to come from the script. It's always been like that. Always."

Nevertheless, Freeman's talent is indisputable. His work is considered impeccable by many of the professionals with whom he has worked. Edward Zwick, the director of *Glory*, believes that "Morgan inhabits a role rather than performs it." The actor himself agrees, saying that you must let yourself "inhabit" your character and "reach whatever depths a character has." The finest actors, he says, demand their audiences' attention. "Audiences believe what you believe," he says. "It's a matter of believing yourself. If I believe me, then you've got no choice. None at all."

Although few fans or directors who have worked with Freeman would believe that there are roles he cannot play, Morgan believes that being a talented actor also means knowing one's limitations. Freeman refuses to play certain roles—for example, Abraham Lincoln—because he believes they are beyond his range.

Freeman may not have wanted to portray Lincoln, but in 1998 he became president of the United States—in the movie *Deep Impact*. The film is an apocryphal tale about a comet's collision with earth and the choices people make as the disaster nears. Although it suffered somewhat at the box-office from

its similarity to the Bruce Willis blockbuster *Armageddon*, which opened just a few months later, Freeman earned praise for his portrayal of the fatherly, reassuring President Beck. "You find yourself hoping that when Armageddon arrives, somebody as sensible, humane, and good-fatherish as Morgan Freeman is in the White House," wrote Richard Schickel in *Time* magazine. "Freeman should run for president after playing the perfect one here," Leah Rosen of *People Online* enthused. The actor received a 1999 NAACP Image Award nomination for Outstanding Supporting Actor in a Motion Picture.

Less successful was Morgan's appearance in *Hard Rain* (1998). Departing from his usual "good-guy" roles, Freeman played the sinister leader of a group of villains in a small Midwest town. The men plot to rob

Morgan Freeman has never been afraid to take diverse roles. In 1998, he played both the president of the United States (in Deep Impact, *shown here) and the mastermind of a $3 million robbery in* Hard Rain.

an armored car of $3 million. The gang is determined to carry out the heist despite a torrential rain that floods the town. But the result, *People* magazine declared, was "pretty humdrum, apart from a couple of outlandish action sequences." Freeman "[brought] a grumpy dignity to his role," the reviewer continued, but "*Hard Rain* was shot in a gigantic [water] tank, and it looks it."

What's in Morgan Freeman's future? Plenty. He will reprise his *Kiss the Girls* character, Dr. Alex Cross, in *Along Came a Spider*, based on the 1993 thriller by James Patterson about the search for two kidnapped school girls. He will also appear in *Nurse Betty*, a comedy costarring Chris Rock and Renee Zellweger, in which Freeman is one of two hit men who try to kill a woman they believe has witnessed them at work. Scheduled for release in December 1999 is the film *Rendezvous with Rama*, based on a novel by Arthur C. Clarke. Freeman is Commander William T. Norton, the leader of a crew sent into space to explore man's first encounter with alien intelligence. Also slated for 1999 are *Water Damage*, which began filming in Toronto in December 1998; *Long Way to Freedom*, directed by Shekhar Kapur, who also directed the historical film *Elizabeth* (1998); and *Under Suspicion*, directed by Stephen Hopkins and costarring Gene Hackman.

In addition to motion picture roles, Freeman directed the made-for-television movie *Mutiny*, which aired in March 1999. He also said in a recent interview that he is at work on another directing project, *A Day No Pigs Would Die*. The film is an adaptation of a story about growing up during the Great Depression.

What does Morgan Freeman do when he is not performing? Aside from acting, his one passion is sailing. He finds peace on the water, and he takes his boat out at every opportunity. One of the few extravagances he has allowed himself was to purchase in

1970 a 30-foot sloop (a small, single-masted boat), which he named the *Lenora II* after his maternal grandmother. Freeman taught himself how to navigate by the stars, and he sails regularly in the Caribbean. He has sailed to the Florida Keys, Bermuda, and as far north as Nova Scotia. After his stage run with *Driving Miss Daisy*, he took a cruise to St. Lucia in the British West Indies with his wife and granddaughter.

Freeman now owns a 38-foot ketch (a two-masted vessel with a large foremast and a smaller aftermast), which he has named the *Sojourner* after

Freeman attends the 67th Annual Academy Awards ceremony in 1994 with his wife and daughter. Despite the accolades he has received from fans and critics, the actor claims not to put too much stock in awards and honors. "Fame isn't what you want," he says. "What you want is to work."

the 19th-century abolitionist and women's rights crusader Sojourner Truth. Before the release of *Amistad* in December 1997, Freeman took the *Sojourner* to Trinidad, where he planned to spend a few months taking a break from work. When the "right" role comes along, Freeman says, he knows it, and he simply "ties up the boat" and goes home to work.

Morgan's wife, Myrna Colley-Lee, compares his love for sailing with his determination as an actor: "That man loves to dream—on the stage, on [the computer] screen, and at sea." But sailing also offers a refreshing dose of reality for a man who spends much time in the "make-believe" world of acting. "I feel insignificant here in Hollywood," he once said. "When you live in the world of make-believe, you need something real; I go sailing, I'm in the real world."

The reality of sailing can be much more challenging—and harrowing—than the dreamy, beautiful world of birds and wind that one might imagine. On one trip, Freeman says, he was aiming for Sable Island in the North Atlantic, some distance from Nova Scotia, but he never reached it. He and his wife encountered a storm that lasted more than a week. Myrna became so dehydrated that "she became delusional," Freeman recalls. Did he call for help? "No, I didn't call the Coast Guard," Morgan snaps. "The reason you go out there is to try to deal with [problems yourself]." A former neighbor who has known Freeman for several years says that "Morgan's sailing is part of his 'loner/Western' side." The neighbor's daughter added that "Morgan likes power. Sailing is a control kind of sport."

When not sailing or working, Freeman spends time horseback riding on his 44-acre ranch near Charleston, Mississippi. The ranch was his family's property; after the death of his stepfather in 1990,

Freeman moved back to his home state. "I lived 25 years in New York," he says, "and after a while I began to know that every time I went into a building, I was going into a big cave. I lived on the third level of a cave that had almost no natural light. So I gave that up. Literally said 'This is it. I'm out of here. Going to where the sun shines all the time.'" Freeman relishes the South, where people have "a certain sense of community, a respect for fellow man. . . . We're blessed with not having to deal with the anonymity of numbers" that urban dwellers often contend with.

Freeman is decidedly private about his personal life, particularly about his first wife and his children. He and Myrna are presently raising their granddaughter, E'Dena Hines, the daughter of Freeman's adopted daughter Deena. Along with his daughter Morgana, he also has two sons, Alphonse and Saifoulaye, by women he did not marry.

Does Morgan Freeman's suddenly hectic work schedule ever get him down? "You ought to be glad about your life, whatever it is," the sixtyish actor says. "I've got all my fingers and toes. My eyesight is good. My smeller works. Of course I'm happy about my life, because I'm still here." About his fame as an actor, Morgan remains realistic. He has no regrets about his late rise to major motion picture status. After all, he believes, the real test of success is how hard and how well you work. "You don't want to spend your life worrying that you're going to lose it. . . . Fame isn't what you want. Stardom isn't what you want. That's the result. What you want is to work, isn't it?"

CHRONOLOGY

1937   Morgan Freeman born on June 1 in Memphis, Tennessee, to Mayme Edna
        Revere Freeman and Morgan Porterfield Freeman

1939   With sister, moves in with Evelyn Freeman, paternal grandmother, in
        Charleston, Mississippi

1943   Evelyn Freeman dies; Morgan moves to Chicago to live with parents and cousins

1944   Moves with mother and sister to Greenwood, Mississippi, to live with maternal
        grandmother, Lenora Greenlee Revere

1946   Returns to Chicago with mother and sister; performs *Little Boy Blue* at school

1948   Moves to Gary, Indiana, then returns to Greenwood, Mississippi; President
        Harry S Truman orders integration of armed forces

1950   Wins first acting medal in Mississippi state competition

1955   Graduates from high school; enlists in the U.S. Air Force (discharged in 1959)

1961–62 Travels to New York City, then San Francisco; performs in *Threepenny Opera*

1963–64 Appears as dancer at the New York World's Fair

1967   Performs in summer stock theatre, Stowe, Vermont; marries Jeanette Adair
        Bradshaw

1969   Appears in Bertolt Brecht's *In the Jungle of Cities*, Boston; George Farquhar's *The
        Recruiting Officer*, Philadelphia; and B. J. Friedman's *Scuba Duba*, New York

1971–76 Appears as Easy Reader on public TV's *The Electric Company*

1978   Wins Clarence Derwent Award, Drama Desk Award, and a Tony nomination
        for performance as Zeke in *The Mighty Gents*; appears in *White Pelicans* with
        José Ferrer

1979   Lands title role in the New York Shakespeare Festival's *Coriolanus*; appears in
        TV's *Hollow Image*; divorces Jeanette Adair Bradshaw

1980   Wins Obie Award for performances in *Mother Courage and Her Children* and
        Coriolanus; appears in films *Brubaker* and *Attica*

1982   Plays Othello and the Duke of Florence (*All's Well That Ends Well*) at Dallas
        Shakespeare Festival

1982–84	Appears as architect Roy Bingham in *Another World* (daytime soap opera)
1983	Marries costume designer Myrna Colley-Lee; stars in *The Gospel at Colonus*, for which he wins an Obie Award
1984	Films *Harry and Son* with Paul Newman
1987	Films *Street Smart*, which earns him awards from the New York Film Critics Circle, the Los Angeles Film Critics, and the National Society of Film Critics, as well as nominations for Academy and Golden Globe Awards; stars as Hoke Colburn in off-Broadway run of *Driving Miss Daisy*
1988	Wins an Obie for stage performance in *Driving Miss Daisy*; appears in *Clean and Sober* with Michael Keaton
1989	Appears in *Lean on Me* and *Johnny Handsome*; movie version of *Driving Miss Daisy* nominated for an Academy Award; appears in *Glory*
1990	Appears in Shakespeare in the Park production of *The Taming of the Shrew* and film *The Bonfire of the Vanities*
1991	Costars with Kevin Costner in *Robin Hood: Prince of Thieves*
1992	Films *Unforgiven* and *The Power of One*
1993	Directs his first project, *Bopha!*, starring Danny Glover and Alfre Woodard
1994	Costars in *The Shawshank Redemption*, for which he is nominated for Oscar, Golden Globe, and Screen Actors' Guild Awards
1995	Appears in *Outbreak* with Dustin Hoffman and *Seven* with Brad Pitt
1996	Films *Moll Flanders* and *Chain Reaction*
1997	Costars with Ashley Judd in *Kiss the Girls*; appears in *Amistad*, directed by Steven Spielberg
1998	Costars with Christian Slater in *Hard Rain*; appears as President Beck in *Deep Impact*
1999	Directs made-for-TV movie *Mutiny*; stars in big-screen films *Along Came a Spider*; *Long Way to Freedom*; *Nurse Betty*; and *Rendezvous with Rama*

Morgan Freeman as the sophisticated Moor, Azeem, in the 1991 epic Robin Hood: Prince of Thieves.

FILMOGRAPHY

Film

Who Says I Can't Ride a Rainbow? (1971)

Coriolanus (1979)

Julius Caesar (1979)

Brubaker (1980)

Death of a Prophet (1981)

Eyewitness (1981)

Harry and Son (1984)

Teachers (1984)

Marie (1985)

That Was Then, This Is Now (1985)

Street Smart (1987)

Clean and Sober (1988)

Driving Miss Daisy (1989)

Glory (1989)

Johnny Handsome (1989)

Lean on Me (1989)

The Bonfire of the Vanities (1990)

Robin Hood: Prince of Thieves (1991)

The Power of One (1992)

Unforgiven (1992)

Bopha! (director, 1993)

The Savior is Born (voice, 1993)

A Century of Cinema (as himself, 1994)

The Shawshank Redemption (1994)

Outbreak (1995)

Seven (1995)

Chain Reaction (1996)

Cosmic Voyage (voice, 1996)

Moll Flanders (1996)

Amistad (1997)

Kiss the Girls (1997)

The Long Way Home (voice, 1997)

Screening (as himself, 1997)

Deep Impact (1998)

Hard Rain (1998)

Along Came a Spider (1999)

Long Way to Freedom (1999)

Nurse Betty (1999)

Rendezvous with Rama (1999)

Under Suspicion (1999)

Water Damage (1999)

Television

The Electric Company (series, 1971–76)

Wonder Woman (series, 1976)

Roll of Thunder, Hear My Cry (1978)

Hollow Image (1979)

Attica (1980)

The Marva Collins Story (1981)

Another World (series, 1982–84)

The Atlanta Child Murders (1985)

The Execution of Raymond Graham (1985)

The Twilight Zone (series, 1985)

Resting Place (1986)

Fight for Life (1987)

Clinton and Nadine (1988)

The Civil War (miniseries, voice of Frederick Douglass, 1990)

The Promised Land (voice, 1995)

Mutiny (director, 1999)

Stage

Threepenny Opera (1961–62)

The Royal Hunt of the Sun (1966)

Hello, Dolly! (1967)

The Niggerlovers (1967)

A Taste of Honey (1967)

In the Jungle of Cities (1969)

The Recruiting Officer (1969)

Scuba Duba (1969)

Caught in the Middle (1969–70)

Black Visions (1972)

Sisyphus and the Blue-Eyed Cyclops (1975)

Cockfight (1977)

The Mighty Gents (1978)

White Pelicans (1978)

Coriolanus (1979)

Julius Caesar (1979)

Mother Courage and Her Children (1980)

All's Well That Ends Well (1981)

Othello (1981)

Buck (1983)

The Gospel at Colonus (off-Broadway, 1983)

Driving Miss Daisy (1987)

The Gospel at Colonus (Broadway, 1988)

The Taming of the Shrew (1990)

BIBLIOGRAPHY

Abele, Robert. "Morgan Freeman." *US* magazine, May 1997.

Adero, Malaika. *Up South: Stories, Studies and Letters of This Century's African-American Migrations*. New York: The New Press, 1993.

Associated Press. "Morgan Freeman, An Actor in Working Progress," *USA Today*, 19 December 1997.

Cooper, Jeanne. "Formidable Morgan Freeman." *Washington Post*, 26 April 1993.

Craig, Jeff. "Thrill Seeker: Morgan Freeman Returns to Suspense in *Kiss the Girls*." *Hollywood Boulevard* (Internet), 20 September 1997.

Dudar, Helen. "For Morgan Freeman, Stardom Wasn't Sudden." *New York Times*, 10 December 1989.

Feingold, Michael. "Morgan Freeman Tames the Shrew." *Village Voice*, 24 July 1990.

Gates, Anita. Review of *Seven*. *New York Times*, 1 October 1995.

Grossman, James R. *Land of Hope: Chicago, Black Southerners, and the Great Migration*. Chicago: University of Chicago Press, 1989.

Guerrero, Ed. *Framing Blackness: The African American Image in Film*. Philadelphia: Temple University Press, 1993.

Harrington, Richard. "Morgan Freeman Meets His Match." *Washington Post*, 3 March 1989.

Hill, Michael E. "The Narrator Has His Own Story to Tell." *Washington Post*, 12 February 1995.

Kael, Pauline. Review of *Glory*. *New Yorker*, 5 February 1990.

———. Review of *The Bonfire of the Vanities*. *New Yorker*, 14 January 1991.

Lane, Anthony. Review of *The Shawshank Redemption*. *New Yorker*, 26 September 1994.

Lemann, Nicholas. *The Promised Land: The Great Black Migration and How It Changed America*. New York: Alfred A. Knopf, 1991.

Lombardi, John. "Morgan Freeman in the Role of His Lifetime." *Esquire*, June 1988.

Maslin, Janet. Review of *Outbreak*. *New York Times*, 10 March 1995.

———. Review of *Seven*. *New York Times*, 22 September 1995.

Nichols, Peter M. Review of *Outbreak*. *New York Times*, 19 March 1995.

Rhines, Jesse Algeron. *Black Film/White Money*. New Brunswick, NJ: Rutgers University Press, 1996.

Simpson, Janice. "In the Driver's Seat: Actor Morgan Freeman Eases into High Gear." *Time*, 8 January 1990.

Snead, James. *White Screens, Black Images: Hollywood from the Dark Side*. Colin McCabe and Cornel West, eds. New York: Routledge, 1994.

Szymanski, Michael. "Morgan Freeman Waxes Profound About Acting, *Kiss the Girls*, Kim Basinger, and the Rest of the Known Universe." *Mr. Showbiz* (Internet), 1997.

Trescott, Jacqueline. "Actor Morgan Freeman Can Take His Pick of Roles. And He Has." *Washington Post*, 10 December 1997.

Whitaker, Charles. "Is Morgan Freeman America's Greatest Actor?" *Ebony*, April 1990.

INDEX

PICTURE CREDITS

GINA DE ANGELIS holds a B.A. in theater and history from Marlboro College, Vermont, and an M.A. in history from the University of Mississippi. She has lived in Australia, was a professional actor at the Pennsylvania Renaissance Faire, and writes drama as well as nonfiction. *Morgan Freeman* is her third of 12 books for Chelsea House.

NATHAN IRVIN HUGGINS, one of America's leading scholars in the field of black studies, helped select the titles for the BLACK AMERICANS OF ACHIEVEMENT series, for which he also served as senior consulting editor. He was the W. E. B. DuBois Professor of History and Afro-American Studies at Harvard University and the director of the W. E. B. DuBois Institute for Afro-American Research at Harvard. He received his doctorate from Harvard in 1962 and returned there as professor in 1980 after teaching at Columbia University, the University of Massachusetts, Lake Forest College, and the California State University, Long Beach. He was the author of four books and dozens of articles, including *Black Odyssey: The Afro-American Ordeal in Slavery*, *The Harlem Renaissance*, and *Slave and Citizen: The Life of Frederick Douglass*, and was associated with the Children's Television Workshop, National Public Radio, the Boston Athenaeum, the Museum of Afro-American History, the Howard Thurman Educational Trust, and Upward Bound. Professor Huggins died in 1989, at the age of 62, in Cambridge, Massachusetts.